I Love You Already

By Lyn Wells Clark

Illustrated by

James Seger

This book is dedicated to my grandsons,
Tate and Cole Macdonald.
Thank you for all the love and light you bring in to my world.

I Love You Already

By Lyn Wells Clark

Illustrations by James Seger

Published by Blue-Eyed Star Creations, LLC and Carolyn Clark

2 Old Forest St., Middleton, MA 01949

lynwellsclark.com

2024 Blue-Eyed Star Creations LLC and Carolyn Clark

All rights reserved. No portion of this book may be reproduced in any form without permission from publisher, except as permitted by U.S. copyright law.

For permissions visit lynwellsclark.com

ISBN: 979-8-89316-164-9 - hardcover

ISBN: 979-8-89316-165-6 - paperback

ISBN: 979-8-89316-166-3 - ebook

I love you already.
Can't wait to see
your face.

We'll be fast friends.
We'll laugh and play.

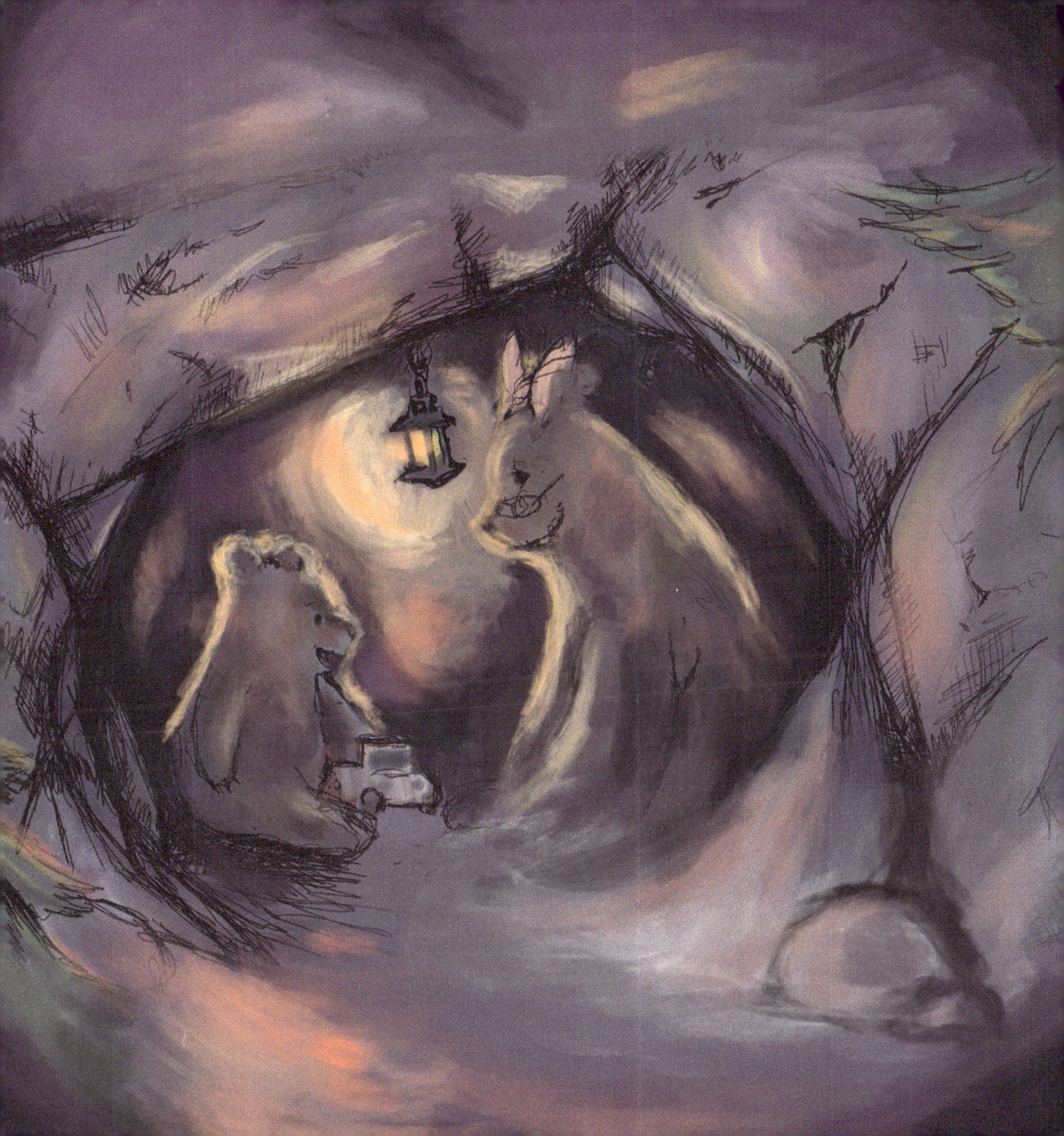

Whether near or far this holds true...

my sweet grandchild,
I will always love you.

Welcome to the family, little one!!

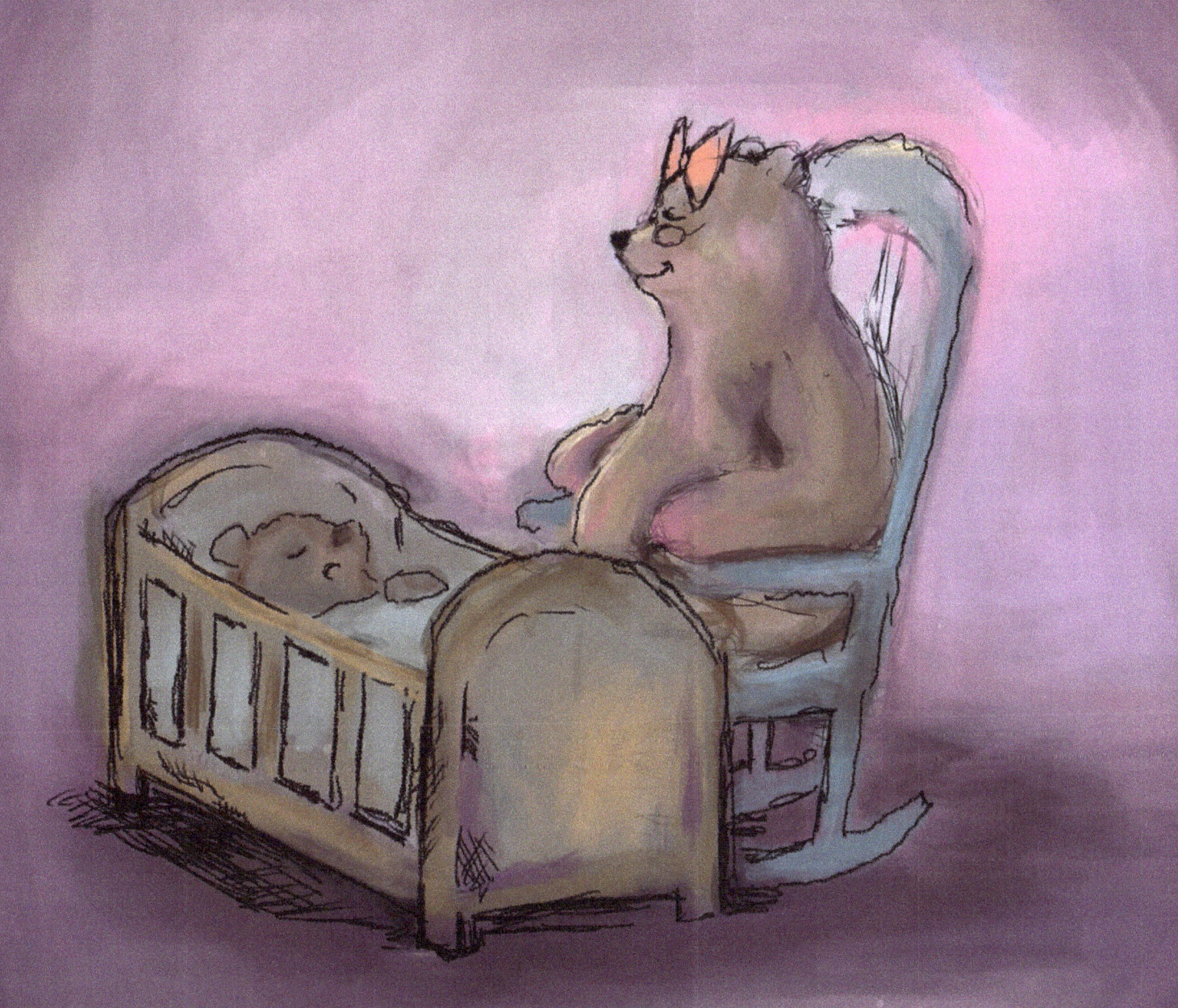

Much love and gratitude to my wonderful husband and children. Thank you for your love, support and inspiration.

OTHER BOOKS BY THIS AUTHOR

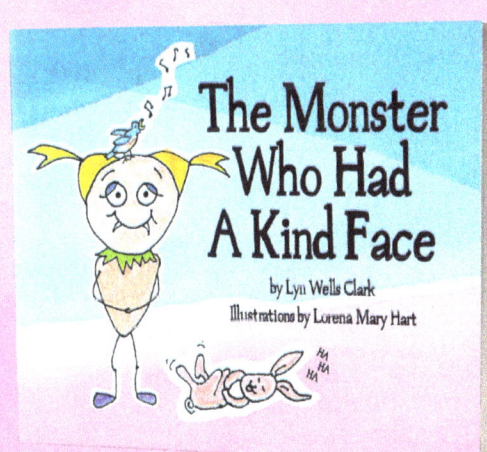

Many thanks to up and coming illustrator James Seger for his outstanding effort in bringing this story to life.

ABOUT THE AUTHOR

As the author of six children's books, Lyn Wells Clark is actively pursuing her dream of becoming a successful author. Lyn's most recent book, I Love You Already, is inspired by and dedicated to her beautiful grandbabies.

Lyn believes that it is never too early to begin conversations of kindness and each of her books reflects that belief.

Lyn's other passions include pickleball, yoga and a love-hate relationship with the game of golf.

For information on all of Lyn's books, you can visit her website, lynwellsclark.com.

www.ingramcontent.com/pod-product-compliance
Lightning Source LLC
Chambersburg PA
CBHW061350010526
44107CB00011B/895